AF865804

Rebuilding Our Democracy

A 96-Year-Old Veteran's Plan to Revitalize the Country,

With the Numbers to Back It

Lawrence A. Yaggi Jr.

Rebuilding Our Democracy

A 96-Year-Old Veteran's Plan to Revitalize the Country, With the Numbers to Back It

First edition, 2026.

ISBN: 979-8-9883842-6-7

Published by lyaggi.org Press, Roseburg, Oregon

Printed by IngramSpark.

Contents

Acknowledgments

My son David read every page of this book before anyone else did, as my editor and as a stand-in for the reader I wrote it for. His questions, the ones I could answer and the ones I could not, sharpened the argument and kept me honest. Whatever errors remain are mine. The book is better for his hand.

Preface

THE COUNTRY'S LIST OF BROKEN THINGS IS LONG, and I want to say at the outset that no single book is going to fix all of it. I am one retired engineer at one kitchen table, not a government, and the honest thing to do before I begin is to admit the size of what I have left out.

The list runs long. The office that runs the schools. The foundation that funds the science. The foreign service, the veterans' agency, the postal service, the tax service, the corps that organizes national service. Each of these has been cut or hollowed in its turn, and each deserves a careful repair of its own. I touch some of them in these pages and pass others by, not because they do not matter, but because one book cannot carry them all and still be read.

So, I had to choose where to start, and I started with two things, because they are the two that everything else stands on. The first is what it costs to live, the price of a house, a prescription, a month of childcare, a tank of gas. The second is trust, whether the people in charge can be believed, or whether they are mostly busy serving themselves. I have come to think these two are the foundation. Fix them, and you earn the standing to take on the rest. Leave them broken, and nothing else you propose will get a hearing, because no one is listening.

That is what this book tries to do. It is not the whole repair. It is a place to begin; a set of fixes aimed squarely at bringing down the cost of living and rebuilding a government people can trust again. There are many more repairs the country needs, and a good number of them matter as much as these. I have simply started where the pain and the distrust run deepest.

The method, though, does not change from one repair to the next, and it is the one thread I would ask you to carry from the first page to the last. Rebuild the broken thing. Modernize it while you are at it. Right-size it honestly, taking seriously the argument that it had grown too large. And then judge it by the only test that matters, whether it serves people better than before, and not merely whether it is back.

What follows is one citizen's list, with the costs filled in and a number on every fix. I offer it the way an engineer offers a drawing, to be checked, argued with, corrected, and added to. The country has no shortage of broken things. What it has been short of is people willing to pick up the tools.

CHAPTER ONE
The Habit of Fixing Things

I SPENT MY WORKING LIFE as an engineer and as a financial officer. In both of these professions, there is one lesson you never unlearn. When a machine or a financial system stops working, you do not stand over it and shout. You do not blame the machine or the system for being what it is. You find the defect. You isolate it, you understand why it failed, and only then, once you know the cause, do you fix it.

I am ninety-six years old. For most of those years I fixed systems that had stopped working, first in engineering and later in finance, and I was good at it for one reason. I followed that rule without exception. You do not get to skip the diagnosis because you are angry, or because you already have a culprit in mind. The machine does not care who you blame. It answers only to the cause.

Late in my life I have now pointed that same old habit at the thing that had come to trouble me more than any broken machine ever did. I pointed it at my own party, the Democratic Party, and at the country it is supposed to serve. I had watched something fail that I did not understand, and a man who has spent a lifetime finding defects cannot simply walk past this one. So, I did what I have always done. I gathered the data before I let myself form an opinion.

What I found was not the thing either side was shouting about. I found that people had stopped believing anyone in charge was on their side. Not the other party. Anyone. That is a different kind of failure, and it calls for a different kind of repair. That is the defect this whole book sets out to repair, and it is worth naming plainly before we go a step further. Not a country that picked the wrong party, but a country that has stopped believing any party is on its side.

* * *

I want to be plain about who is writing this, because it should shape how you read it. I am a Democrat, and this book is hard on Democrats in places. It is hard on Republicans too, but I did not write it to win an argument with the other party. I wrote it because the party I belong to has a problem it has not been honest with itself about, and you cannot fix a problem until it is named.

So, let me tell you the method, because the method is the whole book. Every proposed fix in these pages is built the way I would write a specification, not the way a campaign writes a slogan. A slogan states a goal. "We will make life more affordable." That is a wish, not a plan, and an engineer would slide it back across the table. A specification states four things. It names a specific problem. It offers a credible solution, with the actual mechanism and not just good intentions. It puts a believable timeline on the work. And it commits to a measurable outcome, a number you can check later to see whether the thing actually worked.

A specific problem. A credible solution. A believable timeline. A measurable outcome. I call it the HOPE formula, because those four parts together are what real hope is built on, the kind a person can check instead of a promise they are asked to swallow whole. I hold every fix in this book to it. If a fix cannot meet that standard, it does not belong in a plan. It belongs in a speech as a promise.

There is one more rule running underneath all of it, and it is the hardest one to keep in politics. Name the cause, not the culprit. People have had a bellyful of blame. We turn on the television, and someone is being blamed, and it changes nothing on the kitchen table. When the grocery bill climbs, we do not need a villain. We need to know why it climbed, and what would bring it down, and when. Costs rise for nameable reasons, and nameable reasons have remedies. A culprit only gives us someone to be angry at.

Out of all of it, the message comes down to a few plain words. We will make it work. We will make it honest. We will make it affordable. Make it work, a government that answers the phone and does its job. Make it honest, a government that is not busy selling itself. Make it affordable, which is the one thing every kind of voter in this country is asking for at the same time. Those three lines are the refrain you will hear throughout this book, not as slogans, but as the headings every fix is filed under. Three fixes, and behind each one a specification you can hold me to.

And over all of it, one line more, because it is the opposite of what people have come to expect from politics. Restoration, not revenge. I am not writing to punish anyone. I am ninety-six. I have neither the time for it nor the taste for it. I am writing to restore some things that have been broken. Lower costs. A hospital that keeps its doors open. An office that answers when a widow calls about her Social Security. A government that works and does not sell itself. Alliances repaired across a table instead of in a courtroom. A country put back into working order rather than turned against itself. That is the spine of everything that follows.

* * *

I have laid the book out the way I would lay out any repair. First the diagnosis, an honest look at what actually failed and why both parties earned the distrust they are living with. Then the record, what each side has really done across my lifetime, so the diagnosis rests on facts a skeptic can check and not on my say-so. Then the repair itself, a set of costed, specific fixes sorted by what can be done in one session, in one term, and over one decade. Then the harder question, how do you rebuild a hollowed-out government without turning vengeful in the process of doing it. And last, the one place where all of it either lands or it does not. A single rural Oregon county, my own, turns out to be a faithful mirror of a thousand communities like it across the country.

I did not set out to write a book. I set out to find a defect. The book is what the diagnosis became once I followed it all the way down.

So, let me start where any honest repair has to start. Not with the fix. With finding the defect.

Your Notes — Chapter One

Your Notes—Chapter One

CHAPTER TWO

Finding the Defect

I BEGAN WHERE I HAVE ALWAYS BEGUN, with the numbers, before I let myself decide what they meant. The first one stopped me cold.

As I write this, in the summer of 2026, about one American in ten approves of the job Congress is doing. Something close to **86%** disapprove. When I went looking for how many people still trust the government in Washington to do the right thing most of the time, the figure was near **17%**. I am old enough to remember when that number was **77%,** back in 1964. In one lifetime, mine, the country's faith in its own government fell by sixty points.

Now, a number like that is easy to misread, and the misreading is where most of politics goes wrong. You could look at it and conclude that people have soured on one party and are waiting for the other to come and rescue them. That is not what the data says. Both parties are underwater at the same time. My own party's favorability sits near 28%, the lowest it has been in about thirty-five years, and the Republicans are only modestly better. The persuadable voter has not weighed two trusted options and found one of them wanting. They have looked at the whole works and decided it is broken.

That is the defect, and it changes everything about the repair. If people believed one party worked and the other did not, the cure would be easy. You would make the case that the other party is worse. But you cannot win back someone who has lost faith in the car itself by telling them the other mechanic is worse than you. They have stopped believing that any of you can fix the car.

* * *

So, I kept gathering data, because "the whole works is broken" is a complaint, not a diagnosis. A diagnosis names the specific failures. I found four, and they fall into a clear order, with one standing well above the rest.

The first, and the largest by a wide margin, is the cost of living. When voters are asked what will decide their vote, more name affordability than name democracy, immigration, and crime combined. Two out of three say Washington has delivered them no relief at all. Most telling of all, more than a third of the people who voted for President Trump in 2024 say the cost of everyday life is now the worst they can remember. This is not a partisan complaint. It is the complaint, the one thing the whole country is saying at once.

A Democratic pollster named Stanley Greenberg put his finger on my own party's share of the blame. For years, he said, Democrats kept insisting the economy was strong while hardly any of their candidates would say the plain word "affordability" out loud. You do not have to be a pollster to know how that lands at a kitchen table where the groceries cost more every month. The strong economy was on the chart. It was not in the cart.

And here the discipline from the last chapter earns its keep. The cost of living did not climb because of a villain. It climbed for nameable reasons: tariffs on imports and on building materials, an energy shock in 2026 tied to the conflict with Iran, and a sweeping new federal law that pushed health costs higher. Name the cause and you can find the fix. Name a culprit and all you have is someone to be angry at. I will come back to every one of those causes later, each with a fix attached. For now, it is enough to say that the biggest grievance in the country is also among the most fixable, once you are honest about why it happened.

The second failure is that Congress looks out for Congress. Ask Americans whether members of Congress and their families ought to be allowed to trade stocks while they write the nation's laws, and something near nine in ten say no, and they say it together: about 87% of Republicans, 88% of Democrats, 81% of independents. I have studied a great many polls in my time, and I cannot recall a question that united people like that one. It was the single most popular reform anyone tested. And yet it took years, and a procedural maneuver to force it onto the floor, before Congress would so much as vote on it. A congressman from Maine, Jared Golden, said the plain thing out loud, that members should not use their seats to line their own pockets. When the most popular idea in the country is the one the Congress least wants to touch, you have found the cleanest example of the disease. This is what "make it honest" is for.

The third failure is my own party's, and I will not soften it. The Democratic brand is broken. Favorability near 28%, the lowest in thirty-five years, and confidence in the party's congressional leadership at the lowest point ever recorded. James Carville, who was winning Democratic campaigns before some of today's strategists were born, called his own party a "cracked-out clown car," and complained that it speaks to ordinary people in faculty-lounge words like "intersectionality" that mean nothing at a bus stop. Now, Carville is not despairing, and neither am I. He points out that the party keeps winning actual elections, in Omaha, in Virginia, in New Jersey, and in Wisconsin. That tells you something important about the defect. It is not that Democrats cannot win votes. It is that they have lost trust even while they win votes, which means the trouble is the message and the brand, not the turnout. It is fair to ask whether the real failure is the messaging or the governing behind it, and the honest answer is both. A party that does not deliver earns the distrust it gets. But the gap I am naming here is the brand, because even a record that delivers counts for little once people have stopped believing it. The protest vote is landing on them by default. It will not stay unless they give it a reason to.

The fourth failure belongs to the Republicans, and it is the opening. A real share of the people who voted for President Trump in 2024 already regret it, something like one in eight, against roughly one in sixteen of the people who voted the other way. The regret runs heaviest among the young, among Hispanic voters, and among lower-income voters, the very people whose votes had widened his coalition. About one in five of his voters without a college degree say they are finished with the Republican Party. Younger voters have swung hard the other way. Even a Republican strategist, Ford O'Connell, conceded that holding the House in 2026 would take an all-hands-on-deck effort.

But I owe you the honest caveat, because it is nearly the whole ballgame. Regret is not attached to anything. Ask the regretful Trump voters what they would do instead, and they scatter in three directions. The swing among the young is a swing against whoever is in charge, not a swing toward the Democrats. The door is open. Nobody is walking through it yet. It opens only for the party that credibly owns the three things the country is asking for, and that explains the causes instead of pointing at a culprit.

* * *

When I laid the four failures side by side against the people who feel them, one thing jumped off the page.

Group	What they care about most	What lands hardest
Democratic voters	The cost of living, housing, health-care costs, rule of law	**Affordability**, and the party's own broken brand

Group	What they care about most	What lands hardest
Independents (the voters who decide elections)	The cost of living, threats to democracy, corruption, a competent government	**Affordability**, and a Congress that serves itself
Persuadable Republicans	Prices, tariffs and trade, the deficit, the price of gas	**Affordability**, traced to its causes, not to the person they voted for
Younger voters (18 to 29)	Affordability, housing and jobs, climate	**Affordability**, in a politics that must be earned, not assumed

Read down the last column. Every group, the Democratic base, the independents who decide elections, the persuadable Republicans, the young voters who came and went, names the cost of living. Affordability is the only grievance shared by all four. This is not a talking point. This is the spine the whole forward plan is built with, the one repair that speaks to everyone at once.

Put the four failures together and the disaffected voter, the one neither party has won, stops being a mystery. They are not asking either side for more ideology. They are asking, in plain order, for three things: a government that works, a government that does not sell itself, and a government that makes daily life affordable. Said the way a campaign would say it, they come out as a few plain words.

We will make it work.
We will make it honest.
We will make it affordable.

The party that credibly owns those three, instead of running on "the other party is worse," wins the bloc that decides the election. I am convinced of it.

But I am an engineer, and I have already told you what I think of a slogan. Three plain words you cannot check are just another promise, and the country has had its fill of promises. Before I have any right to turn these into fixes you can hold me to, I owe you the evidence first. The record of what each party has actually done, across my lifetime, so you can test my diagnosis against the facts and not against my feelings. That is the next chapter, where I lay the whole record on the table.

Your Notes — Chapter Two

CHAPTER THREE

The Record

I PROMISED YOU THE RECORD, so here it is, and I mean to lay it out the way an engineer lays out test results, the specification on one side and the measured outcome on the other, with no thumb on the scale.

Every record has to start somewhere, and the honest place to start is 1980, because that is where the two parties as we know them, today, took their modern shape. The Democratic framework descends from the New Deal and the Great Society, from the idea that the federal government should stand as an active guarantor of a family's economic security. Social Security in 1935, Medicare and Medicaid in 1965, the Affordable Care Act in 2010, they are all the same template, broad social insurance paid for federally. The Republican framework as we know it crystallized with Reagan's win in 1980: lower marginal tax rates, lighter regulation, a smaller domestic federal footprint, a larger defense, and, over the years, a remade judiciary.

I want one thing understood before a single law goes on the table. These are not a good party or a bad party. They are two honest theories of what a government is for, and as you are about to see, each one delivers on type. The moment you treat the other party's theory as a crime, you have left diagnosis behind and gone hunting for a culprit, the very thing I said at the start I would not do. The record does not need a villain. It needs to be read.

* * *

There is one difference between the two sides that turns up before you read a single law, and it shapes how the rest of this chapter has to be read. One party runs on a record. The other runs on a promise. You can see it in their own 2024 platforms. The Democratic platform is a long, conventional document built largely around what the Biden-Harris administration had already done. The Republican platform is a different animal, about sixteen pages against the sixty-six of 2016, opening with twenty numbered promises, reading closer to a rally speech than a policy paper.

Neither approach is wrong, but the two call for different tests. You judge a record by what it delivered. You judge a promise by whether it was kept. So, for the party that ran on promises I have put a promises-kept accounting in the back of the book, where it belongs, and here I will hold both sides to the same plain question. What did the thing actually do?

* * *

Start with my own party, because a man ought to audit his own books first. Here is the Democratic record since 1980: the major laws, what each set out to do, and what the measured results show.

Law and year	What it set out to do	What actually happened
American Recovery and Reinvestment Act (2009)	Stop the Great Recession's free-fall and save jobs.	About $787 billion in tax cuts, state aid, and infrastructure. CBO credits it with raising 2009 employment by 0.6 to 1.6 million and GDP by 1.2% to 3.2%. Debated, but credited with cushioning the fall. (CBO)
Affordable Care Act (2010)	Move toward near-universal coverage and end pre-existing-condition denials.	Marketplace subsidies, optional Medicaid expansion, consumer protections. The uninsured rate fell from 15.5% in 2010 to a record-low 7.9% in 2023; about 20 million adults gained coverage. (Census; HHS; CBPP)

Law and year	What it set out to do	What actually happened
Dodd-Frank and the CFPB (2010)	Prevent another 2008-style crash and protect consumers.	Created the Consumer Financial Protection Bureau, bank stress tests, and the Volcker Rule. The CFPB reports more than $21 billion in relief to over 205 million consumers since 2011. (CFPB)
Expanded Child Tax Credit (2021)	Cut child poverty with a larger, fully refundable credit.	A one-year expansion to $3,600 per young child, paid partly monthly. Child poverty fell to a record-low 5.2%, nearly halved in a year. It expired after 2021, and child poverty more than doubled, to 13.7% by 2023. (Census; Columbia; ITEP)
Infrastructure Investment and Jobs Act (2021, bipartisan)	Rebuild roads, bridges, broadband, water, and the grid.	About $1.2 trillion, the largest infrastructure investment in decades. Thousands of projects funded nationwide, outcomes still rolling out. Passed with Republican votes. (CRS; DOT)
CHIPS and Science Act (2022, bipartisan)	Rebuild domestic semiconductor manufacturing.	About $52.7 billion in incentives plus a manufacturing tax credit. Private commitments tied to CHIPS have topped $600 billion across roughly 130 projects in 28 states. (Harvard Kennedy School; industry data)
Inflation Reduction Act (2022)	Lower drug costs, let Medicare negotiate prices, invest in clean energy.	A $35 monthly insulin cap and a Part D out-of-pocket cap for Medicare, plus the first-ever Medicare price negotiation. The first ten negotiated prices take effect in 2026, at least 38% below 2023 list prices. (CMS; KFF; AARP)

Read down the columns and you see one theory at work, the New Deal idea carried down the decades and, of late, pushed into industrial policy with the semiconductor and infrastructure laws. But the most honest single piece of evidence in this whole chapter is the Child Tax Credit of 2021, and it is honest precisely because it came with an off switch. For one year the country paid families a larger, fully refundable credit, and child poverty fell to the lowest level ever recorded, nearly cut in half. Then the measure expired, and child poverty more than doubled, climbing back to 13.7%. You almost never get to watch cause and effect that plainly in public policy. The policy worked. And then my own party let it lapse, which is a fair thing to hold against us, and I will come back to it.

* * *

Now the Republicans' books, held to the very same question.

Law and year	What it set out to do	What actually happened
Economic Recovery Tax Act (1981)	Spur growth by cutting high marginal tax rates.	An across-the-board cut of about 23% to individual income-tax rates. It defined the supply-side era; growth returned mid-decade alongside large deficits and a 1982 partial rollback. Causes still debated. (historical record)
Welfare reform, PRWORA (1996, bipartisan, signed by Clinton)	Move recipients from welfare to work and end the AFDC entitlement.	Replaced AFDC with the time-limited, work-conditioned TANF block grant. Caseloads fell about 60% from 1994 to 2004. Contested: the block grant's real value has eroded by about a third. (Brookings; HHS)

Law and year	What it set out to do	What actually happened
Bankruptcy Abuse Prevention Act, BAPCPA (2005)	Curb perceived Chapter 7 "abuse" and make filing harder.	A means test and higher filing costs steered filers toward Chapter 13. It caused a large, permanent drop in Chapter 7 filings; NY Fed research found the decline raised insolvency and foreclosure among the most distressed. (NY Fed)
Deregulation, the "two-for-one" order (2017)	Cut regulatory burden: repeal two rules for each new one.	Agencies were directed to net-reduce costs. The administration claimed billions in savings; Brookings and others faulted the method for ignoring foregone benefits. Judged real but modest. (OIRA; Brookings)
Tax Cuts and Jobs Act (2017)	Boost growth through lower business and individual rates.	Cut the corporate rate permanently from 35% to 21%; individual cuts set to expire end-2025. CBO found about a 0.7% average annual GDP boost but a deficit rise of roughly $1.1 to $1.4 trillion over a decade. No model found it paid for itself. (CBO; JCT; Tax Policy Center)
Judicial appointments (2017–2020)	Reshape the federal judiciary.	Three Supreme Court justices confirmed, plus a large slate of lower-court judges. In 2022, Dobbs overturned Roe, making the "leave it to the states" abortion posture operational. (Supreme Court record)

Law and year	What it set out to do	What actually happened
One Big Beautiful Bill Act, OBBBA (2025)	Make the 2017 cuts permanent, cut spending, end taxes on tips and overtime.	Extended the 2017 cuts (about $4.5 trillion) and made the largest Medicaid cut in the program's history. CBO: about $3.4 trillion added to deficits through 2034; roughly 11.8 million more uninsured by 2034, partly offset by $50 billion in rural-hospital relief. (CBO; CRFB; CRS)

Here too the theory is coherent down the years, lower rates, lighter regulation, a smaller domestic government footprint, with the judiciary and the 2025 law carrying that frame into health and social policy. And here too one pattern repeats plainly enough that even the party's own scorekeepers do not dispute it. Three times, in 1981, in 2017, and in 2025, the rates were cut. Three times the deficits rose. And three times the nonpartisan analysts, the Congressional Budget Office among them, found that growth never grew enough to pay back the lost revenue. You may argue the tradeoff is worth it, and many do, but the deficit numbers themselves are not in question.

* * *

So, lay the two records side by side and read them the way you would read a test report on your own design, looking for what is true and not for what flatters you. I read a great many such reports in my working life. The page never cared which design I was proud of. It told me what passed and what failed, and a good engineer learns to read the failures first. I have tried to read both these records the same way. Two weaknesses stand out, one to a side.

On the Republican side it is arithmetic, the recurring gap between the promise that growth will pay for the tax cut and the columns that show it did not. On the Democratic side it is follow-through, the working policy left to die.

The Child Tax Credit is the clearest case. It was written as a one-year measure, its extension passed the House, and then it stalled in a Senate split fifty to fifty for want of a single vote, so a policy that had just halved child poverty simply lapsed. One side will not face its own arithmetic. The other will not finish what works.

And there are two places where honest people genuinely disagree, and I will not pretend they do not, because the fastest way to lose a thoughtful skeptic is to settle on the page a question that is not settled in the field. Welfare reform in 1996 is read by some as a success that moved people from welfare to work, and by others as a cut whose real value has eroded for thirty years. The 2017 tax law's growth claims are credited by some economists and doubted by others. I give you both sides. I do not hand you a verdict, because the record does not contain one.

That is the record, as plainly as I know how to lay it. Two theories of government, each delivering on type, each carrying a weakness it would rather you did not notice. I did not put it in front of you to crown a winner. I put it there so that when I start naming fixes in the next chapter, you will know they did not come out of my prejudice. They came out of the evidence. So, to the repairs the country actually needs, and the order they have to come in.

Your Notes — Chapter Three

CHAPTER FOUR

A Plan to Fix, With Numbers

YOU HAVE SEEN THE WHOLE WORKS JUDGED BROKEN, and you have seen the record behind it. This is the chapter where the book stops describing the trouble and starts repairing it.

Everything that follows is built to one rule, the same rule I laid down at the start. A fix names a specific problem. It offers a credible mechanism, the actual lever that moves the thing, not a good intention. It carries a believable timeline. And it commits to a measurable outcome, a number you can check later to see whether it worked. A specific problem, a credible solution, a believable timeline, a measurable outcome. If a repair cannot meet that standard, it is not in this chapter.

The hope is in the sorting. You do not fix a country all in one motion, that is how people look at the size of the job and give up. You sort the work by when it can honestly be done. Some of it a single session of Congress could pass without first winning the White House, through bipartisan votes, a deal, or plain public pressure, and a strong showing in the 2026 election would only widen that opening. Some of it needs the whole government, a congressional majority and the presidency won in 2028, and can be done inside the term that follows. And some of it is the slow, structural kind that takes a decade of steady building. That middle piece of the formula, the believable timeline, is the framework of this chapter, and affordability comes first in every part of it, because affordability is the one thing the whole country is asking for at once.

I want to be plain about why this is hope and not a wish, because the difference is the whole point. Every fix below names the bill or the mechanism, the cost, and a number you can hold Congress and the administration accountable to. Some are already moving through Congress.

One has 86% of the country behind it. One has already worked once, and we watched it work. This is not a dream list. It is a work order.

One Session, *what a single Congress could pass now*

These are the repairs that do not have to wait for a new president. Some already have the votes and need only a floor vote, the stock-trading ban that most of the country wants, a housing bill that has cleared the Senate, a child-credit fix that has cleared the House by better than five to one. Others are more contested, and those move one of two ways. They get folded into a bill that has to pass anyway, a budget or a debt-ceiling deal, where a Congress that changed hands in 2026 holds real leverage. Or the pain does the work: when premiums spike on a senator's own voters, signing the fix costs a president less than vetoing it. None of this needs a clean sweep. It needs bipartisan votes, a deal, or pressure that lands where it is felt. That is where belief gets built.

1. Restore the health-insurance credits. When the enhanced Affordable Care Act premium credits lapsed at the end of 2025, marketplace premiums jumped by an average of 114%, more than a thousand dollars a year, and about four million people are headed for the uninsured rolls. Restoring the credits costs roughly $31 billion, and the size of the premium spike gives it a real chance this session, because the pain is landing on voters in both parties. The measure: those four million stay covered, and the premium hike is rolled back.

2. Cap insulin and drug costs for everyone. The 2022 law capped insulin at $35 a month and out-of-pocket drug costs at $2,000 a year, but only for people on Medicare. Everyone else is still exposed. Extend the same two caps to private insurance. The measure: the share of insulin users paying more than $35 falls toward zero.

3. Ban members of Congress from trading stocks. Nothing feeds the sense that Washington serves itself like lawmakers trading the stocks of companies they regulate. About 86% of the country wants it stopped, Republicans and Democrats alike, and a bill to do it is already moving. Ban members and their families and require them to divest within three to six months. The measure: full compliance, and trust in Congress tracked to see whether it climbs.

4. Pass the housing and child-credit fixes already on the table. Two repairs are already sitting in Congress with broad support. One housing bill passed the Senate without a single no vote. A child-tax-credit fix passed the House 357 to 70. Pass them. The measure: more housing units built, and about sixteen million children getting the fuller credit in the first year, several hundred thousand of them lifted out of poverty.

5. Stop price-gouging and junk fees. Part of what makes daily life cost more is hidden, junk fees tacked onto bills and price-gouging on essentials. A federal anti-gouging law and a rule against junk fees would pull those costs back into the open. The measure: documented fee reductions, and enforcement actions brought.

One Term, *what a governing majority could do*

The next set needs an election won first, a majority in Congress and the presidency to go with it. These are bigger, but every one of them is the work of a single term, not a generation.

6. Bring back the full Child Tax Credit. This is the one we already watched work. When the 2021 version was in force, child poverty fell to 5.2%, the lowest ever recorded. When it lapsed, poverty more than doubled. Restore it in full, fully refundable, paid monthly, at a cost near $100 billion a year. The measure: child poverty cut by more than 40% again, back toward 5%.

7. Make the health credits permanent and negotiate more drug prices. One-session patches are temporary by design. Make the Affordable Care Act credits permanent and lift the limit on how many drugs Medicare is allowed to negotiate each year, so far it has negotiated only its first ten. The measure: the uninsured rate held at or below its record low near 8%, and the list of negotiated drugs growing.

8. Cap the cost of childcare. Childcare now runs past $13,000 a year for one child in much of the country, up about 30% since 2020, while millions of families cannot find a slot at any price. Cap what a family pays at nearly 7% of its income, and invest in building more supply, the way several states already have. The measure: childcare as a share of family income, and new slots opened against the shortage.

9. Reverse the Medicaid cuts and save the rural hospitals. The 2025 law cut Medicaid by about a trillion dollars, putting the coverage of roughly ten million people and a great many rural hospitals at risk, a Medicaid figure smaller than the near twelve million in Chapter Three, which counts everyone the law pushes off coverage of any kind. Restore the funding and make rural-hospital support permanent, not the temporary patch the law left behind. The measure: coverage restored toward where it was, and rural hospital closures averted. This one comes home to my own county, and I will return to it.

10. Write sensible rules for artificial intelligence. The technology is moving faster than the law. With no federal floor, the harms land on ordinary people: fraud and deepfake scams that hit seniors hardest, threats to children, lost jobs, and even electricity bills driven up by data centers. Set a federal floor, safety and transparency for high-risk systems, protection for children, real anti-fraud rules, while letting states go further if they choose. The measure: a law with a real floor, a measured drop in AI-enabled fraud losses, and data-center power costs kept off household bills.

One Decade, *the structural repairs*

The last set is the patient kind, the repairs that take more than one vote and more than one term and have to be built up steadily across years. They are no less concrete for being slow. Each still names its mechanism and its measure.

11. Close the housing gap. The country is short three to four million homes, and most households can no longer afford a typical new one. The single biggest obstacle is local rules on what can be built where. Tie federal building incentives to states and towns that reform their zoning and permitting, expand the low-income housing credit, and make room for manufactured housing. The measure: housing starts up, the shortage closed over the decade, and rent eating a smaller share of income.

12. Rebuild and modernize the agencies. The offices that answer the phone, inspect the food, chase the fraud, and forecast the storm have been hollowed out. The fix is not to rebuild them exactly as they were, but to bring them back leaner and smarter, with modern systems and a standing team in each one asking what it actually needs to do its job. The measure: faster service and better results than before, not merely a return to the old baseline. The full blueprint is the next chapter.

13. Build energy abundance to bring costs down. The 2026 energy shock helped push inflation back up, and the grid is strained by surging demand from data centers. Build out the grid and generate more power from every source, with the largest energy users paying their fair share of the cost. The measure: household energy costs bending down, and new capacity added to the grid.

14. Make the math honest. The tax cuts of 1981, 2017, and 2025 each widened the deficit, the last one alone by about $3.4 trillion, pushing the debt toward 124% of the size of the whole economy. The fix is not "tax the rich." It is everyone paying a fair share: close the loopholes and carve-outs that let some avoid paying and tie any future cut to a way of paying for it. The measure: the debt, set against the economy, bending downward over the decade.

15. Rejoin the world on climate, and restore what was torn out. At the start of 2026 the United States left the Paris climate agreement, standing now with Iran, Libya, and Yemen as the only nations outside it. Rejoin it, restore a responsible climate-finance commitment, and rebuild the clean-energy and science capacity that was cut. Sell it for what it plainly is: wildfire protection, honest disaster forecasting, healthier forests, and clean-energy jobs in rural counties. The measure: back in the agreement, the science restored, and clean-energy jobs recovered.

16. Restore the Voting Rights Act safeguards. Since a 2013 Supreme Court ruling, a key protection of the Voting Rights Act has sat dormant, and places with a history of violations can change voting rules or redraw maps close to an election with no advance review and little public notice. Pass the John Lewis Voting Rights Advancement Act: restore that review and require any change to voting rules to be announced at least six months before an election. The measure: the protection restored, and the advance-notice rule in force before the 2028 election.

* * *

Sixteen fixes, and not one of them a stray item, because they sort cleanly under the same three words the diagnosis handed us. Make it affordable covers most of them, the health credits, the drug caps, the Child Tax Credit, childcare, Medicaid, housing, and energy. Make it honest covers the stock-trading ban, the crackdown on gouging and junk fees, honest math on the deficit, a real floor under artificial intelligence, and fair voting rules announced in advance. Make it work covers the rebuilt agencies, the rural hospitals, the housing we actually build, the power we actually deliver, and the climate science we restore. The message and the plan are not two things. They are one thing, said two ways.

That is the plan. Sixteen repairs, each with a bill or a mechanism behind it, each with a number you can hold Congress and the administration accountable to, each sorted by when it can honestly be done. None of it requires a miracle, just serious analysis and honest negotiations. Some of it is already moving. One piece of it has already worked once. That is what I mean by hope. Not a feeling that things will turn out fine, but a work order with the costs filled in and a date you can check it against.

The largest item on that list, rebuilding the agencies that were hollowed out, carries a danger folded inside it. Do it in anger, and you have not restored a government, you have only changed whose hand is on it. So, the next chapter is about how you rebuild without becoming the thing you replaced. Restoration, not revenge, and what that actually takes.

Your Notes — Chapter Four

CHAPTER FIVE

Rebuild Without Revenge

I ENDED THE LAST CHAPTER ON A WARNING, and I want to begin this one by taking it seriously. The largest repair on the list is rebuilding the parts of the government that have been hollowed out, and that repair carries a danger folded inside it. A government can be hollowed out by one side and then turned into a weapon by the other, and the people watching from their kitchen tables cannot tell the two apart, except that the second crowd promised to be better. If renewal is only revenge in a clean shirt, the persuadable voter knows it, and they will not hand you their trust, because they have seen this picture before and they know how it ends.

So, this chapter is about how you rebuild a government without becoming the thing you replaced. The name for it, the line that runs underneath the whole book, is restoration, not revenge. It is the harder road, and it is the only one that earns the trust back.

* * *

The discipline that keeps accountability from curdling into revenge is a simple sorting test, and it is the keystone of everything in this chapter. A persuadable voter will not trust a blanket "lock them up," and they will not trust a blanket "let it all go" either. They want the honest middle, a line drawn case by case that they can actually defend. So, you sort every action that was taken into one of three tiers, and the tier decides the remedy.

Tier	What it covers	The remedy
Tier 1 *Lawful but damaging*	Policy choices made by lawful means: tax and program cuts, deregulation, lawful staff reductions, budget caps.	Win elections and reverse them the same lawful way, through legislation, rulemaking, and budgets. No investigations. This is politics, not crime.
Tier 2 *Contested legality*	Actions whose legality is genuinely in question whether or not a challenge has yet been brought.	If a court or watchdog is already reviewing it, let them finish. If none is yet, bring the question to one. Restore whatever they order and prejudge nothing.
Tier 3 *Clear illegality*	Acts a court has actually found unlawful. Nothing reaches this tier on our own say-so.	Accountability through the established legal channels, with full due process, and only where a finding supports it. Never as payback.

Look hard at that top row, because most of what was done lives there. The tax cuts, the program cuts, the deregulation, the lawful staff reductions, the great bulk of the grievance is Tier 1, lawful but damaging. And the remedy for Tier 1 is not a courtroom. It is an election. You win, and you reverse the policy the same lawful way it was made. That is the most important sentence in this chapter, because it is the one that separates renewal from revenge. What was done by lawful means gets undone by lawful means, at the ballot box and in the committee room, not in a cell. Only at the bottom, where a court has actually found that a line was crossed, does the law itself step in, and even then only with due process, and never as payback. A persuadable voter can stand behind a line drawn like that. They cannot stand behind "lock them up," and they should not be asked to.

One more thing about the chart, because it is a snapshot of a moving picture. An action does not sit in one tier forever. The ones whose legality is in doubt begin in the second tier, contested, and often not yet challenged at all. The honest response is not to brand them illegal and jump them to the third, because that shortcut is exactly what a politics of revenge would take. We do the reverse. Where we believe a line was crossed, we carry the question to a court or a watchdog and let the finding, not our certainty, decide. An act becomes a third-tier matter only when a court says so, and not one day sooner. One caveat belongs here, because a referee is only as good as their independence. Where a judge or official had a hand in the very actions under review, the answer is the ordinary one, recusal and conflict-of-interest rules, so a clean hand makes the call. That is a standard applied case by case, not a purge of the judges we would rather not face. That patience is not weakness. It is the whole difference between accountability and revenge.

* * *

With that line drawn, you can pick up the tools. But there is a right way to rebuild and a wrong way. The wrong way is to put the government back exactly as it was, brick for brick, and call that a victory. The right way is to rebuild and modernize at the same time, to bring each office back leaner and smarter than it was, with up-to-date systems and a standing habit of asking what it actually needs to do its job well.

And here is where the honest negotiation happens. The Republicans have argued for years that government had grown bloated, slow, and too fond of its own size. On a good many days, they have a point. So, we do not wave that away. We take it seriously, and we rebuild right-sized, which is common ground, not surrender. A government that works is not the same thing as a government that is large. Say so out loud, and we rebuild it with a majority behind us instead of only our own half.

So, start with the watchdogs, because they are the cleanest common ground of all. The inspectors general, the in-house auditors who hunt waste and fraud, were fired in a single night early in 2025, and a court has since ruled that firing unlawful. Those were the very people who had turned up billions of dollars in fraud. Fill the vacancies through the lawful process, restore their funding and grow it a little, and give them modern data tools to catch fraud faster. Restoring the fraud-catchers is the anti-waste agenda the Republicans say they want, so there is no cleaner place to begin. The same goes for the consumer watchdog that had returned more than $21 billion to ordinary people since 2011, shuttered and gutted and now tied up in court. Restore its funding, staff it to its mission and no larger, and modernize how it handles complaints.

Then the service desk. There is an office that answers when a widow calls about her Social Security, and it has been cut to where the wait can run into hours, while a report that told the truth about those waits was altered to look better and the watchdog who wrote it was fired. Restore the staffing, modernize the phone lines and the website, and tell the public the honest numbers again. An office that answers the phone is not a luxury. It is where "make it work" is kept or broken, one call at a time.

Then the agencies that watch the sky and guard the body. The weather service that warns a county a storm is coming lost hundreds of forecasters, and the labs that sharpen the forecast were slated to close. As one objection put it plainly, weather forecasts are not waste, fraud, or abuse. The same sky carries our air travel, and the agency that keeps the planes safely apart, the FAA, runs short not only of controllers but of the modern equipment that safe flight depends on. The medical research that becomes next year's treatments saw its grants cut and thousands of its scientists walk out the door. The agency that keeps the air and the water clean had its scientific core thinned. In each case the repair is the same shape: restore the capacity, modernize the tools, and bring honest science back through the front door.

And then the bridge to the rest of the world. The agency that carried American help abroad was cut to almost nothing. Here the right-size question is sharpest, and the honest answer is not to rebuild the old footprint but to stand up a leaner, modern capacity aimed at the programs that measurably save the most lives. That agency is also the hinge into the second half of this repair, the one that happens not at home but across our borders.

The list runs longer than these, the schools office, the science foundation, the foreign service, the veterans' agency, the postal service, the tax service, the national-service corps, each cut or hollowed in its turn. The principle does not change from one to the next. Rebuild it, modernize it, right-size it honestly, and judge it by whether it serves people better than before, not merely by whether it is back.

* * *

This carries us across the border, to the alliances and the trade that were strained alongside the agencies. And here there is some good news hiding in the shape of the problem. Almost all of the damage abroad is Tier 1, lawful but damaging choices about tariffs and trade. And Tier 1, you will remember, is repaired by negotiation, not by a courtroom. There is a table to sit at, and a place to start.

Start from the common ground, because there is more of it than the headlines suggest. About 85% of the trade between the United States and Canada was already eligible to move without tariffs under our shared agreement, and after a call between the two leaders in the summer of 2025, Canada lifted the retaliatory tariffs it had placed on compliant American goods. The Canadian prime minister described it as the two countries re-establishing free trade for the vast majority of their goods. So, you begin the conversation from that 85%, not from the handful of bitter disputes. An honest footnote belongs here: the 85% is the share eligible to move tariff-free, and the share that actually does is lower, so closing that gap is itself a shared, winnable goal, the kind both sides can claim credit for.

There is even a table ready and waiting. Our trade agreement with Canada and Mexico comes up for its required joint review this very summer, the natural moment to reset the relationship with our two closest neighbors and largest trading partners. On the Canadian side, the prime minister has already seated a bipartisan advisory council that includes members of the opposition party, which is the negotiated-common-good model in plain action, the other country showing us the very thing this book is asking for. The disputes that remain, the tariffs on autos and steel and aluminum and lumber, you negotiate down through that review. You do not re-litigate them.

And the same restoration logic reaches the climate table. At the start of 2026 the United States left the Paris climate agreement, standing now with a very short list of nations outside it. You rejoin it, and you rejoin the larger climate convention, and you restore a responsible commitment, for the same reason you negotiate the trade back: because standing with your neighbors is worth more than standing apart, and because the science you rebuild at home, the forecasters and the labs, is the same science that does the work.

* * *

So, all of it, at home and abroad, resolves into a single posture, and it is worth saying plainly, because it is the opposite of what people have come to expect. We are not committing to purge anyone. We are not committing to prosecute our way back to a working country. We are committing to four things. To rebuild a government that works. To take the Republicans' argument about its size seriously, and rebuild it leaner, which is common ground and not surrender. To let the law, and not our anger, settle who actually crossed a line. And to negotiate our alliances and our trade back to health, starting from the ground we already share.

That is what a working two-party democracy is supposed to look like, and it is the cleanest contrast I can draw with the politics we have now, the black-or-white tug-of-war where every question has exactly two answers and the other side is always the enemy. Restoration is slower than revenge, and it is less satisfying on the night of the election. But it is the only kind of repair that is carried out, because it is the only kind the other half of the country can live with.

I have laid out the diagnosis, the record, the fixes, and the rebuild. There is one thing left to do, and it is the thing an engineer always does last. You take the design down off the drawing board and you test it in the field, in one real place, with real people, and you watch whether it holds. For me that place is a single county in rural Oregon, the one I live in, and it turns out to be a faithful mirror of a thousand counties like it. That is the last chapter.

Your Notes — Chapter Five

CHAPTER SIX

One Rural County as a Mirror

I HAVE SPENT FIVE CHAPTERS at the level of the whole country, and an engineer does not trust a design until he has tested it in the field, in one real place, with real people. So, I want to bring all of it home, to the place I live, a single county in the timber country of southern Oregon. Douglas County is not a special case. It is the case. It is exactly the rural, older, cost-pressed, Medicaid-leaning community this whole plan was built for, and that is precisely why it makes a fair test. If the fixes land here, at this kitchen table, in this town of Roseburg, they land in the thousand counties and towns across America that look just like it. This county is a mirror. It is also one of the places carrying the heaviest share of the country's pain right now, and that is exactly why it is the right place to test the plan, because if you want to know whether a repair brings real relief, you try it where the hurt is severe. So, this chapter is not a tour of how bad things have gotten. It is a tour of what relief looks like when it finally arrives.

* * *

Start with the roof over a family's head. This is timber country, it has cut and milled lumber for generations, and yet the tariffs on Canadian lumber have added thousands of dollars to the cost of building a new home right here, in the very place that knows wood best. Here is the relief: bringing that trade relationship back into repair, the patient work of negotiation I described earlier, is how those thousands come back off the price of a house in Roseburg. To the family doing the building, that is not foreign policy. It is the price of a home.

Then the hospitals, because there are only two in a county larger than some states, and about a quarter of the people here are covered by the Oregon

Health Plan, the state's Medicaid, which pays a great share of the bill at both. Mercy, in the county seat at Roseburg, is the larger one, a regional center and the second-largest employer around. The other is a small critical-access hospital out on the coast at Reedsport, more than an hour away over the Coast Range, serving the western end of the county that Roseburg cannot reach. Neither one backs up the other. Each is the only hospital its end of the county has, and the smaller, coastal one is the more fragile, the kind that fails first when the money is cut, which is how rural healthcare always unravels, from the edges in. So, here is what restoring the Medicaid funding and making rural-hospital support permanent actually buys this county: both sets of doors stay open, both payrolls keep signing checks, and nobody's nearest emergency room moves an hour farther down the road. Out on the coast, where the nearest emergency room is already an hour over the Coast Range, an open door is not an abstraction. It is a life saved that would otherwise be lost on the drive. In a rural county, that is not a line item. That is relief you can drive to.

Then the people I know best, because I am one of them. A quarter of this county is sixty-five or older, and the typical household that age lives on something close to $49,000 a year. For us, three of the fixes are not policy, they are the week's arithmetic: a Social Security office that answers the phone, a cap on the price of a month of prescriptions, and help with the cost of caring for a husband or a wife who can no longer be left alone. Because that arithmetic is tighter here than in almost any place in the country, the relief from easing it is felt harder here too. The county with the most to lose from the pain has the most to gain from the cure.

There is a newer danger too, aimed straight at that same quarter of the county, the scams that artificial intelligence now makes possible, the cloned voice on the telephone, the fake grandchild in trouble. A federal floor with real teeth against fraud, and rules that keep the data centers from quietly running up the electricity bill, are not a far-off technology debate out here. They are a guardrail around the savings of the people most likely to be targeted, and there is no county where that guardrail does more good.

And there is the fire. This is a fire-prone, flood-prone, forested county, and the eastern end of it lives that truth every summer. A fully staffed weather service that sees the storm and the fire coming, forests that are actually tended, and the clean-energy work that comes with both, are not costs to a county like this. They are protection, and they are paychecks, the kind of rural jobs that land in places exactly like this one.

And underneath all of it runs the oldest grievance out here, the deep rural distrust of a Washington that looks like it is busy serving itself. The relief for that one is not a program, it is proof. Ban the self-dealing, answer the phone, deliver the grant. Trust is not won back with speeches, it is earned back, one delivered fix at a time. "Make it honest" is how you win back a county that long ago stopped listening.

And it is not all grievance out here, because people notice when the government actually works. When our two senators helped land a telehealth grant for that same hospital, it meant a rancher an hour from town could see a doctor over a screen. That is "make it work" showing up where a person can feel it, and a county like this keeps a quiet scorecard of every time it does.

* * *

Now, a plan like this does not travel on its own, and it surely does not travel on the voice of a national party. Out here, the message moves only if the right neighbor carries it, and it has to be a neighbor the listener already trusts. So, the nurse and the people who work at the hospital carry the word on Medicaid and on keeping the doors open, because on a question of health there is no more trusted voice in the county. The owner of the small business on Main Street carries the word on prices and tariffs and the junk fees that nibble at a household budget, because she lives those numbers every month. The retiree carries it to other retirees, on Social Security and drug prices and the scams, because he is living the same week they are. The candidates on the local ballot carry the plainest message of all, that government can simply be made to work, and they answer for it by name to the people they will run into at the grocery store. The faith communities carry the hardest part, the part about the common good and about restoration rather than revenge. And in the tribal communities, the word on rural health travels through voices those communities have long relied on. Match the message to the messenger, and the neighbor to the neighbor, and a national plan becomes a local conversation.

* * *

I have been talking about one county, my county, but I have not been talking only about it, and that is the whole reason for holding it up. Douglas County is not unusual in its troubles. It is ordinary in them. Its people are older than the country as a whole, more rural, leaning on two small hospitals and the memory of a single industry, more exposed to the cost of a gallon of gas and a box of groceries and a month of insulin. There are something like a thousand counties and towns across this country that would know themselves in that description, in Oregon and Pennsylvania and Michigan and on down the list. And here is the thing worth saying out loud: they did not all vote the same way, and it does not matter. A hospital does not ask a county how it voted before it closes, and the cure does not ask either. The lumber tariff falls on every builder, the Medicaid cut empties every rural ward, the scam call reaches every fixed income, whatever color the county wears on the map. This relief is built for the place, not the party. So, when I say the plan was carried into the field and it held, I mean it holds wherever the trouble is, which is to say nearly everywhere that looks like home.

* * *

So, let me end where this book has been headed from the first page. We are not running to punish anyone. We are running to restore, and to bring accountability, not vengeance. To bring down the cost of a house, a prescription, and a month of childcare. To keep a hospital's doors open. To make sure the Social Security office answers when a widow calls about her check. To rebuild a government that works and does not sell itself, to repair our alliances across a table instead of in a courtroom, and to tend the forests and the forecasts and the rural jobs rather than abandon them. That is restoration, and it is the opposite of revenge.

I began this book by telling you that I spent my working life as an engineer and a financial officer, and that when a thing stopped working I did not stand over it and shout, I found the defect and I fixed it. I was an engineer who could not walk past a broken thing. What I found, when I followed the defect all the way down, was not a villain. It was a country that had stopped believing anyone was on its side, and a long list of repairs that needed to be made. This book has been my attempt to make that list honestly, with the costs filled in and a number on every fix.

There is a verse I have carried a long while, from the prophet Micah, that asks what is required of us and answers in six plain words: do justice, love mercy, walk humbly. I can think of no better description of this work, and no better guard against the temptation to turn renewal into revenge. Do justice, by the law and not by the mob. Love mercy, even toward the other half of the country. And walk humbly, because no party holds a monopoly on being right, and the whole repair depends on our remembering it.

The widow is still waiting for someone to answer the phone. Let us be the ones who answer it.

Your Notes — Chapter Six

APPENDIX A

The Promises, Kept and Not Kept

In Chapter Three I drew a line between the two parties. One runs on a record, the other on a promise, and you judge a record by what it delivered and a promise by whether it was kept. I said I had put the promise side of that accounting in the back of the book. Here it is.

The 2024 Republican platform ran on a set of promises rather than a policy record. Below are the central ones, set against the public record as of June 2026. I have scored them the way I would score any test result, by what actually happened and not by what I might wish had happened. Some were kept. Some were not. Several are still in progress. The honest spread, kept and not kept side by side, is the whole point.

Promise (paraphrased)	Status	What the record shows
Seal the border, stop the migrant invasion	**Largely kept**	Border apprehensions about 238,000 in fiscal 2025, against about 1.5 million in fiscal 2024, the lowest since 1970. Pew reports net migration turned negative for the first time in about 50 years. *(CBP, DHS; Pew; AP)*

Promise (paraphrased)	Status	What the record shows
Carry out the largest deportation in U.S. history	**In progress, contested**	About 605,000 formal removals in year one, plus large self-deportation figures. ICE has struggled to sustain its 3,000-a-day target, and the "largest ever" label is disputed against prior single-year records. *(DHS; NBC; NY Post)*
End inflation, make America affordable again	**Not kept so far**	Consumer-price inflation rose to 4.2% in May 2026, the highest since April 2023, amid a 2026 energy shock tied to conflict with Iran. *(BLS; Trading Economics; Statista)*
Large tax cuts, no tax on tips and overtime	**Kept**	Enacted in the One Big Beautiful Bill Act, signed July 2025. *(CBO)*
Make the 2017 tax cuts permanent	**Kept**	Made permanent in the same 2025 law. *(CBO; CRFB)*
Reinstate and expand deregulation	**In progress**	A January 2025 executive order imposes a ten-for-one rule on new regulations. Implementation is ongoing. *(Sidley; CEI)*
Make America the dominant energy producer	**Mixed**	The pro-production agenda advanced, but energy prices spiked in 2026 after the Iran conflict, pushing inflation higher. *(Trading Economics)*

Promise (paraphrased)	Status	What the record shows
Prevent World War III, restore peace in Europe and the Middle East	**Not kept**	The Russia-Ukraine war continues into 2026, and a 2026 confrontation with Iran triggered an energy shock. *(war timeline; NBC; PBS)*
Build a "Golden Dome" missile-defense shield	**In progress**	Initiated by executive order in 2025. In development, not yet operational. *(executive action)*
Close the Department of Education, return it to the states	**Partial, in progress**	The Supreme Court in 2025 let the administration dismantle the department through mass layoffs. Full abolition would require Congress and has not been enacted. *(NPR; NBC)*

Promise (paraphrased)	Status	What the record shows
Use tariffs to revive manufacturing	**Implemented, no revival yet**	Broad 2025 tariffs were imposed, then narrowed after the Supreme Court struck down their emergency-powers basis in February 2026. The goal itself, more factory work at home, has not yet shown up. Manufacturing employment is down about 1% since the tariffs began, and analysts find no reshoring boom in new factory construction. One sentiment index hit a multi-year high in early 2026, and the administration claims a historic comeback, but the jobs and investment data do not yet support it. *(Federal Reserve; Yale Budget Lab; IoT Analytics; AEI)*
Protect Social Security and Medicare with no cuts	**Mixed**	Social Security and Medicare were not directly cut. However, the 2025 law enacted about $1 trillion in Medicaid cuts. *(CBO; CAP)*

Read down the middle column and the shape is plain. Clear wins on the border and on taxes. Mixed or still unfinished on deregulation, energy, deportations, the Department of Education, and the missile shield. Not kept so far on inflation and on ending the wars. And the single biggest tool, tariffs, put in place and then pulled back by the Supreme Court. I am not asking you to be angry about any of them. I am asking you to read it straight. That spread is why some of the people who voted in 2024 already feel they were sold something that did not arrive.

One last gauge deserves a word, because it is the one the administration reaches for most. Ask about the economy and the answer comes back as the stock market, which has climbed to record after record. A rising market is real, and it counts for something. But it is worth asking what is actually rising. Almost the entire climb has come from a single story, artificial intelligence and the data centers built to feed it. AI-related companies drove something like 80% of the market's gains in 2025, and the largest handful of them now make up about a third of its whole value, a concentration not seen since the dot-com peak. That same building boom is holding up a large share of the country's economic growth, by some estimates more than half of it.

So, the index climbs. But a market is not an economy. It measures what investors will pay for a slice of a few enormous companies, and most of those gains land with people who already own the stock. It does not measure the price of a house, or a month of insulin, or whether the rural hospital keeps its doors open. Some of the same analysts watching the market rise warn that it may be hiding a weaker economy underneath, a soft job market and a cost of living that has not let up. A rise in value can make a great market. A great market is not the same thing as a great economy. The promises scored above were made about the second one, and the second one is where they have to be judged. *(Goldman Sachs; Oliver Wyman; Fidelity; CNBC)*

A Note on Sources

I have tried throughout this book to follow one rule about evidence: name the source and lean on bodies whose job is to count honestly rather than to win an argument. Where a number appears, in the record tables, in the appendix, in the figures on cost and coverage, it comes from a named source, cited in place, so that you do not have to take my word for any of it. You can look it up and check me. That is the whole spirit of the thing.

The figures come, first, from the government's own counters and nonpartisan referees: the Bureau of Labor Statistics for jobs and inflation, the Census Bureau for income and poverty, the Congressional Budget Office and the Joint Committee on Taxation for the cost of laws, the Centers for Medicare and Medicaid Services for coverage, the Federal Reserve for output and the broader economy, and Customs and Border Protection for the border numbers. These are the official scorekeepers, and I have used them wherever I could.

Where I have drawn on outside analysis, I have tried to use groups with a record for rigor and to name them plainly: the Congressional Research Service, the Yale Budget Lab on tariffs and the budget, KFF on health coverage and costs, the Center on Budget and Policy Priorities and the Committee for a Responsible Federal Budget on the federal ledger, and Pew Research on public opinion and migration. On the stock market and the artificial-intelligence buildout, I have leaned on research from Goldman Sachs, Fidelity, and Oliver Wyman. For breaking developments I have relied on established news organizations, among them the Associated Press, Reuters, and the major networks.

Two honest cautions. Many of these figures are snapshots, true as of mid-2026 and certain to move, so a reader checking later should expect the numbers to have changed even where the direction has not. And no single source is beyond question. Where it mattered, I have tried to set more than one against another, the way you would check a measurement twice before you trust it. The aim was never to assemble a case for one side. It was to lay the evidence where you can see it and let you judge it for yourself.

About the Author

Lawrence A. Yaggi Jr. is a retired electrical engineer and financial officer, and a Navy veteran of the Korean War. He lives in Roseburg, in the timber country of Douglas County, Oregon. He spent his working life finding why systems had stopped working and repairing them, first in engineering and later in finance, and late in life he turned that same habit toward his own party and the country it serves.

This book grew out of that habit. It is the readable form of a longer work he authored and shared openly, a costed, five-phase strategy framework built on one discipline he calls the HOPE formula: a specific problem, a credible solution, a believable timeline, and a measurable outcome.

He came to the questions of care in this book the hard way. He nursed both of his late wives through long illness, one through breast cancer across a 52-year marriage, the other through more than seven years of Alzheimer's until her passing in 2023. Out of that experience he wrote three books in 2026, each meant to give others the knowledge and comfort he wished he had carried himself: a caregiver's guide to Alzheimer's, a researched companion for the breast cancer journey titled *Knowledge and Awareness Provides Hope*, and a training manual for new hospice volunteers.

The same concern runs beneath this one. He had cared, one person at a time, for the people he loved. This book asks a larger version of the same question, whether a country still takes care of its people, whether the hospital stays open, whether the phone is answered, whether there is help for a husband or wife who can no longer be left alone. He writes not as an expert standing above the reader, but as one citizen who could not walk past a broken thing, offering a drawing to be checked, argued with, and improved.

He is ninety-six.

Your Notes

www.ingramcontent.com/pod-product-compliance
Lightning Source LLC
LaVergne TN
LVHW010740061126
851857LV00014B/1572